KIDDING AROUND

LONDON

A YOUNG PERSON'S GUIDE TO THE CITY

SARAH LOVETT

ILLUSTRATED BY MICHAEL TAYLOR

John Muir Publications
Santa Fe, New Mexico

John Muir Publications, P.O. Box 613, Santa Fe, NM 87504

Library of Congress Cataloging-in-Publication Data
Lovett, Sarah, 1953-
    Kidding around London: a young person's guide to the city
  / Sarah Lovett: illustrated by Michael Taylor.—1st ed.
     p. cm.
    Summary: A guidebook to London's historical, cultural and
recreational attractions.
    ISBN 0-945465-24-6
    1. London (England)—Description—1981- Guide-books—Juvenile
literature. 2. Children—Travel—England—London—Juvenile
literature [1. London (England)—Description—Guides.]
    I. Taylor, Michael, 1953- ill. II. Title.
    DA679.L85   1989   88-43527
    914.21′204858—dc 19   CIP
                                   AC

Typeface: Trump Medieval
Typesetter: Copygraphics, Santa Fe, New Mexico
Designer: Joanna V. Hill
Printer: Eurasia Press Pte. Ltd.
Printed in Singapore

Distributed to the book trade by:
W.W. Norton & Company, Inc.
New York, New York

Special Thanks:
Theo
Jade
Mary St Clair's 6th grade class, Carlos Gilbert School, Santa Fe
Raphael, the coolest, Asana, Lauren, Joanne, and Maloree's
   Junior School, London
Johanna, Tobias, Jemma, Sholla
Karen, Andy, Mali, Alexis
Judy, Brian, David, Charlotte
Drake, Eda, Richard, Al, and Donny
Natalie, Miriam, and Marcia
Joseph and Eleanor Poland
Cathy Wren, Christopher Sykes, Kathleen Raine, Ellen Feldman
Special thanks also to Mara from Michael

Contents

1. Getting to Know London

London is a great city for kids. You can walk underneath a river, get lost in a maze, visit dungeons and torture chambers, edit a film, or watch a laser show. You can see some of the best theater in the world or watch a cricket game go on for five days. You can eat Indian curry hot enough to blow your socks off or munch on English chips and tomato catsup. The only problem is finding the time to do everything.

London is a city filled with tradition. When the pilgrims left England, "the mother country," in 1620 and sailed to Plymouth Rock, London was already 1,577 years old! London has a celebration or a memorial day for almost everything. There's a Druid ceremony to commemorate spring equinox (Druids were the high priests of Celtic Britain). There's a day in memory of Charles Dickens, the famous English author of books like *Oliver Twist* and *Nicholas Nicholby*. And there's even a day when the Lord Mayor of London is presented with a boar's head on a silver platter, a yearly tradition dating back to the twelfth century.

London is the capital of the United Kingdom, which consists of England, Wales, Scotland, and

Northern Ireland. Historically, London dates back a whole lot farther than most cities in the New World. It's more than 1,900 years old. Washington, D.C., the capital of the United States of America, was founded in 1790. Compare the two and London is almost 1,700 years older.

In A.D. 43, Roman invaders founded Londinium (the first name for London) on a sandy stretch of the Thames. Throughout its history, London has been home to kings and queens, artists, and politicians. It's the center of government for Great Britain and also a center for the arts and cultural affairs.

But London has also had its share of hard times. In the ninth century the Vikings, Scandinavian warriors, in their quest for adventure and wealth, cruised up and down the river looting, burning, and generally causing trouble. The Great Plague killed 75,000 Londoners in 1665, and then on Sunday, September 1, 1666, the great fire destroyed 13,000 houses. By 1800, London's population was one million people, the biggest city in the Western world. At that time, boys and girls from the slums worked long hours in horrible sweatshops and factories until child labor laws were enacted at the end of the century. During World War II (1939–1945), more than 30,000 Londoners were killed in the London Blitz when German bombs destroyed much of the city.

London has also been the scene of cultural revolutions like the Beatles and the miniskirt in the 1960s and rockers and punkers in the 70s and 80s.

London is filled with all kinds of people. A lot of them came from other countries like Africa,

Back in the Iron Age (ca.1000 B.C.–A.D. 100), the tribal Celts roamed Europe on horseback. By the fifth century B.C., they controlled central Europe, Britain, and Ireland. Druids were Celtic priests who led religious ceremonies that are believed to have included animal sacrifices and magic.

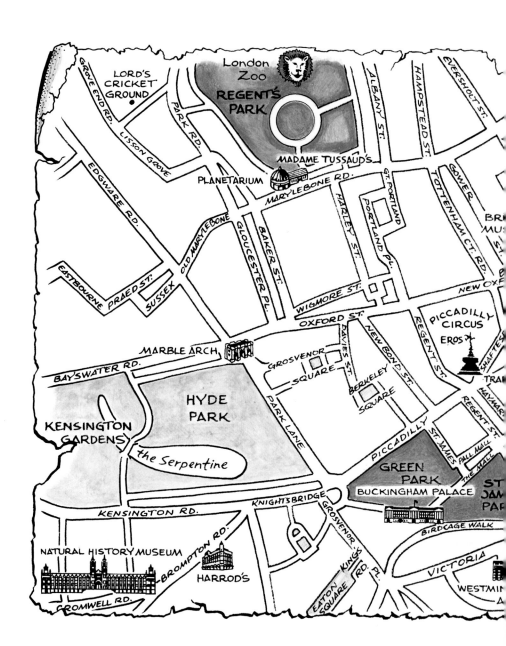

Population of London,
6,765,100. London
occupies 693 square
miles. It is 3,458 miles
from New York and 5,382
miles from Los Angeles.

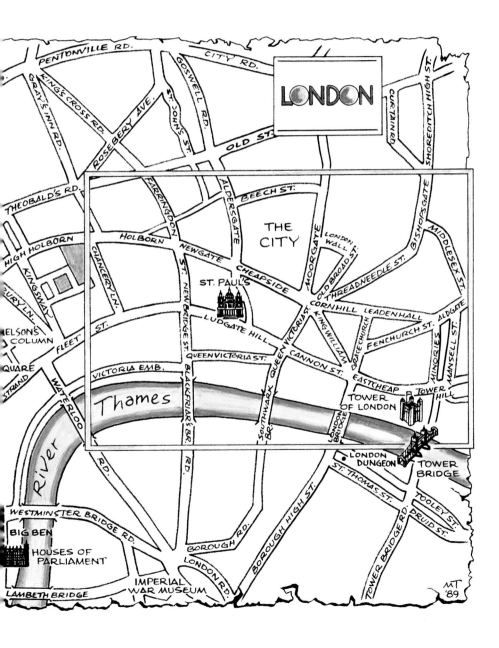

If you get lost or lose the people you're with, always go to the police. If you're in a public building, find a uniformed attendant, or go to the box office, main desk, or information center. If you need emergency help, dial 999 from any phone (it's free) and ask for police, ambulance, or fire. Most of all, keep breathing and don't panic.

Pakistan, India, and the West Indies. You'll hear many different languages spoken on the streets. You'll also see a rainbow of people of every shape and color.

The English really ARE different. Londoners, in general, tend to be very polite for city dwellers. Like most of the English, they don't like to get "too personal." Of course, you'll always find exceptions like "the bloke who's dreadfully rude." And people, especially cabbies, will ask you about your politics.

England has a definite class system with the Royal Family at the top, and then the aristocracy, and it's like a hill that keeps leveling off until you find laborers and new immigrants at the very bottom.

Traveling in another country is a good time to think about your own country—what makes it great and what could be improved. While you're in London, consider the differences between a constitutional monarchy and a democracy.

ROMAN WALL

ROMAN WAITING for TELEPHONE

London is famous for pea-soup fog and rain. It's a good idea to carry an umbrella at all times, but you may find the days are sunny and pleasantly warm depending on the time of year. Rain or shine, it's always humid, and that's probably why London's women are famous for perfect complexions.

London's streets are crowded with buildings. There's not a lot of undeveloped land, but the city is filled with beautiful parks and the vegetation is lush and very green. You'll see a wide range of architectural styles. Older streets might look quaint and picturesque with very narrow houses sharing common walls and lovely gardens. Some of the more recent buildings are just plain ugly with starkly drab exteriors. There's a lot of controversy over London's modern architecture so be careful not to rub that sore spot with Londoners.

London is filled with so many things to do you could spend your whole lifetime exploring. You could take weeks wandering through some of London's museums and still there would be more to see. Traveling in a foreign country is the time to experience diversity, so don't be afraid to try something new. It's a great idea to keep a travel journal. Any old notebook will do. Just carry it along and jot down how things look and how you feel. It's a record of your trip that you can keep for a lifetime.

A word about **how to use this book.** The entries included vary from historical landmarks to sports and entertainment. Entry fees are generally not included because these change so quickly! Free entry is listed. Most fees are under £2 and many are less than 50 pence. Telephone numbers are included because it's always a good

If you travel on London's Underground, you're likely to see "buskers"— musicians who play for spare change and literally sing for their supper. Buskers aren't the only people who "make" their meals in the tube. Like other big cities, London has lots of homeless people. So far, no one has figured out a really good long-term solution for helping them. Maybe you can!

idea to ring first just to double check hours and fees. Chapters are divided by subject so you can pick and choose according to your interests.

England uses a 24-hour clock unlike the United States, which uses a 12-hour clock. When it's 1:00 p.m. U.S. time, it's 13.00 hours in London. Hours in the book are listed first in 24-hour time and then 12-hour time in parentheses.

When possible, any pertinent information concerning special facilities for the handicapped has been included. Again, use the telephone first! You'll find some helpful information on using English money in chapter 9, Shopping, and city transportation in chapter 11, Getting Around Town. Travel is one of the greatest adventures in the world, so have a "smashing" time!

2. Chronology

Saxon
chieftain

A.D. 43—When the Romans conquer Britain, they build a seaport on the Thames near the present-day London Bridge and name it Londinium.

61—The Celtic tribesmen revolt against Nero's Roman rule.

200—The Romans build a wall around Londinium to protect it from raiders.

410—Roman troops withdraw from Britain to protect Italy from invaders.

450—The Angles and the Saxons, two fierce, rival tribes, divide England into separate kingdoms.

825—The Saxons, who control London, gradually unite the rest of England into a single kingdom.

Mid-1000s—King Edward the Confessor, a Saxon, builds a palace and reconstructs a church about two miles southwest of London. Edward's buildings are the beginning of the city of Westminster. The palace serves as the main residence of England's rulers until the 1520s. The church becomes Westminster Abbey.

1066—William the Conqueror, a French nobleman, takes control of England and crowns himself king in Westminster Abbey. He grants London self-government and builds himself a castle, called the White Tower, just outside London to remind Londoners of his power.

1100—London craft and trade guilds develop (Bakers,

King Henry VIII

Queen Elizabeth I

Goldsmiths, Carpenters, etc.). Each guild has special uniforms and meeting halls.

1209—London Bridge, made of stone, replaces wooden bridges used by the Romans to cross the Thames.

Late 1400s—London's population is about 50,000.

1509–1547—King Henry VIII rules England and owns six palaces close to London!

1558–1603—Queen Elizabeth I helps London become an important world trade center.

1577—The first theater, called The Theatre, was opened outside the city walls of London. The crowds were so rowdy they sometimes set fire to the wooden seats.

1599—Shakespeare presents his plays at the Globe Theatre.

Mid-1600s—London's population is 500,000! Most people live outside the city walls. Inside the walls, London is called the City.

1642—Civil war with King Charles I vs. Parliament. London is pro-Parliament, led by Oliver Cromwell and other puritans who oppose the luxury of the Church of England and the noble classes.

1649—The Puritans take control of the government and King Charles I loses his head.

1660—Parliament restores the monarchy and King Charles II is crowned.

1665—The Great Plague, a horrible epidemic of bubonic plague, ravages London and kills thousands of people.

1666, September 2—The great fire of London begins in a baker's shop on Pudding Lane in the City and lasts five days. It destroys most of London, which is made of wood. A total of more than 80 churches and 13,000 houses burn to ashes, but no people are killed!

Late 1600s—London is rebuilt of stone and bricks. The famous architect, Sir Christopher Wren, designs the new St. Paul's Cathedral and many other structures.

1700s—London Stock Exchange is founded on Fleet Street.

1800—London population is one million! It's the biggest city in the Western world.

1800s—The age of the Industrial Revolution. London provides a great market for factory goods.

Mid-1800s—The City's merchants and bankers grow rich, and the West End of London is famous for a glittering social life. Meanwhile, the poor factory workers live in slums in London's East End.

Last half of the 1800s—Reform laws are passed to help the working class.

1840s to 1860s—Railroad stations are built around central London, including Victoria, King's Cross, and Paddington.

1863—London subway system is begun.

1914–1918—WW I. Germany bombs London.

1939–1945—During the summer of 1940, Germany attacks Britain from the air. London is the main target, and the London Blitz lasts from September 1940 to May 1941. Tons of bombs are dropped on the City and the East End. More than 30,000 Londoners are killed during the war and 80 percent of London's houses are damaged or totally destroyed.

1960—Skyscrapers are built in central London.

1962—Beatles.

1967—The miniskirt goes out of style.

1970s—The Punk revolution rocks London.

1988—London's population is 6,765,100.

1860s London Street vendors

London Blitz 1940

John

Paul

George

Ringo

3. Rules and Royalty

ondon has long been the center of Great Britain's ruling powers. Since the Saxons (from Germany) and the Danes (from Denmark) ruled in the ninth century, England's kings and queens understood the need to command London. William the Conquerer began the Tower of London in 1067 for that very reason.

But today, the monarch stands for protocol, ceremony, and the tradition of passing the crown down through the Royal Family. The "doings" of the Royal Family also provide Londoners with lots of entertaining gossip about how princes, princesses, and their friends spend their days.

Parliament is the national legislative governing body of Great Britain. It is composed of the House of Commons, whose members are democratically elected, and the House of Lords, who are usually members by birth. Although politically the House of Lords is somewhat similar to the U.S. Senate, a member of the Senate is elected and a member of the House of Lords is titled either by birth or appointment of the queen. Real political power belongs to Parliament instead of the Royal Family. The prime minister and her or his cabinet rule the roost.

London has more than one kind of royalty! "Cockney" has become a popular term for working-class folks from the East End of London. But true Cockneys must be born within the sound of London's Bow Church bells. Their own royalty, called Pearly Kings and Queens, are famous for special royal suits and dresses covered with thousands of tiny pearl buttons. Although Pearly Kings and Queens have no official political power, they are very important to the Cockneys.

Like America, Britain has two major political parties. Instead of Republicans and Democrats, Britain has the Conservative Party and the Labor Party. But now some of the other parties are getting into the action.

London is divided into boroughs, like mini-governments, and each borough has its own strong political personality. Some boroughs are Conservative and others are Labor.

When you're exploring London, **Buckingham Palace** is a great place to begin. It's the present-day residence of the hereditary monarch, which means the queen lives there when she's in town. Buckingham Palace had its beginnings in the early eighteenth century when the Duke of Buckingham built himself a brick house and called it Buckingham House. Later, George III tore down the library and built a ballroom, but it was George IV who, with John Nash, really went to town on the architecture. Then the king died and Nash found himself out of favor. Later, Victoria moved in as soon as she became queen, and the Royal Standard (flag) could be seen at the Marble Arch. (The Marble Arch was originally built by Nash for Buckingham Palace, but later it was moved to its present spot near Hyde Park.)

These days, Buckingham Palace is the home of Queen Elizabeth. You can tell if she's in residence if the Royal Standard is flying.

Be sure to catch the **Changing of the Guard,** a great ceremony where the old Guard (soldiers who have been on duty) changes with the new Guard. Their scarlet jackets were originally designed to hide bloodstains! The guards change around 11:30 a.m. daily (except September to March, when it happens every other day),

weather and politics permitting. Stand near the Queen Victoria Memorial or the center gates of the palace for the best view. You can always get some information from a policeman if things don't seem to be happening.

Also at Buckingham Palace you'll find the **Royal Mews,** which is a fancy name for a fancy stable. After their wedding, Prince Charles and Princess Diana returned to Buckingham Palace in a glass coach. That very coach is on display. There's also the Gold State Coach (24 feet long, weighing 4 tons) and the Queen's Irish Coach, and you can see the horses, too, unless they're out of the stable. (Wednesdays and Thursdays, 14.00-16.00 [2-4], closed on holidays and Royal Ascot week in June. There's a very small entry fee.)

See if you can pick out the five regiments at Buckingham Palace: white plume, the Grenadiers; scarlet plume, Coldstreams; buttons by threes and no plume, Scots; blue plume, Irish; and green and white plumes, Welsh.

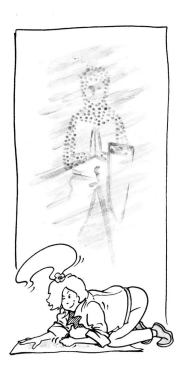

Another hot spot that brass rubbers should check out is St. James's Church, Piccadilly. There you'll find the London Brass Rubbing Centre with loads of brass to choose from. On your hands and knees, you'll rub elbows with knights, queens, judges, and animals, all replicas of old church brass because too much rubbing wears away the details on the originals.

There are 40 acres of gardens at Buckingham Palace, filled with roses, herbs, a lake, and even pink flamingos.

The Houses of Parliament are in a whole different neighborhood. The borough of Westminster covers a lot of the West End of London. **Westminster,** meaning the Houses of Parliament, Whitehall, and such, is the political core of London.

There are so many things called Westminster you might get confused: Westminster Cathedral, Westminster Abbey (an abbey is a church connected with a monastery), Palace of Westminster, Westminster School, and so forth! Even though it's not easy to keep everything straight, there are some great things to explore.

The **Palace** and the **Houses of Parliament** are one and the same, a dignified hodgepodge (Gothic style, which means pointed arches, steep roofs, and sometimes flying buttresses) right next to the Thames. Edward the Confessor (ruler 1042–1066) had the original palace built in honor of the French palaces he admired. Through the centuries, his buildings slowly disappeared because of fire damage and time. In 1835, architects Augustus Pugin and Charles Barry both won a contest for a new palace design. Most of what you see today is their design. You won't be allowed to visit unless you know someone special to arrange a viewing.

William the Conquerer was crowned in **Westminster Abbey** on Christmas day, 1066. Ever since then, it's been the place to be crowned or buried if you're an English sovereign. And yes, you can visit the abbey and you can even use your elbow grease for some nifty brass rubbings of famous people from English history. Choose your favorite brass from around the abbey and then rub the replica. You get paper to put over the brass plaque and special crayons to rub on the paper. (The brass-rubbing center is open daily except Sunday. Abbey open daily 8.00-18.00 [6]. Entry fee. Partly accessible for handicapped.)

Many of London's palaces are no longer used by royalty all the time. Some are museums open to the public, and others are parks. They're usually splendid places to visit.

If you approach the **Tower of London** along the wall of the moat, you can see grass where there used to be water (it was drained in 1843). For hundreds of years the moat was full of filthy water. It was originally supposed to fill with fresh water at high tide and to be cleaned as the tide went out. But the moat was designed lower than the Thames, and it never emptied out. That wouldn't have been so bad except it was loaded

*If you're wandering through **Parliament Square** make sure you look up at **Big Ben.** The clock tower stands 316 feet. The bell was probably named after Sir Benjamin Hall, First Commissioner of Works, and a very massive guy. The bell and clock were finished in 1858-59. When Parliament is "sitting" (in session), a light glows over Big Ben.*

with trash, animal carcasses, and sewage from the town of London. But these days it's a garden.

You can have someone take a photo of you standing next to a Beefeater (a special guard for the tower originally appointed by King Edward VI) at the main entrance. The Beefeaters also offer scheduled tower tours that are fun and interesting.

Located on almost 18 acres of land, the Tower of London is actually many towers linked by walls. It began as a fortress when William the Conquerer wanted to impress the people of London with his power. In later years, the tower was used as the Royal Mint (for making money), an arsenal (for storing weapons), and even a zoo where King Henry VIII kept his exotic animals.

The White Tower, near the center, is the oldest tower of the fortress, dating back to 1078. It took 20 years to build and the walls are 100 feet high. The White Tower houses a collection of lances, crossbows, pistols, and other weapons on the first floor.

The Tower of London is most famous as a prison for political inmates. Those who threatened the king often spent their last days imprisoned inside the fortress.

Don't miss Traitor's Gate where unfortunate prisoners were brought secretly by boat in the dead of night. There's also a wooden execution block and the ax used for beheadings.

One look at the gray stones of the Bloody Tower and you can almost hear the moans and groans of ghostly prisoners. The Bloody Tower got its name from the story of the murder of two little princes. When Edward IV died in 1483, his two sons, twelve-year-old Prince Edward and his

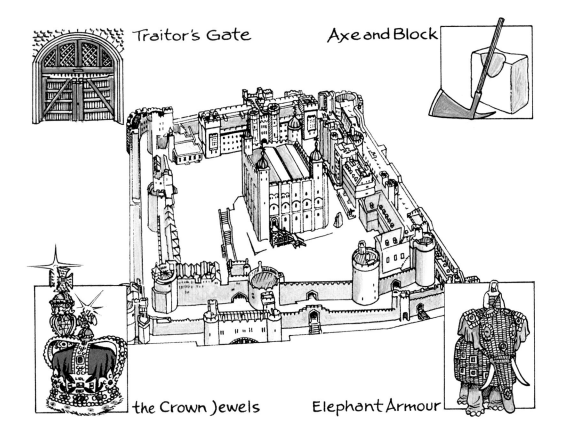

Traitor's Gate

Axe and Block

the Crown Jewels

Elephant Armour

younger brother, were housed in the tower to await young Edward's coronation. But their uncle became king instead (Richard III), and the little princes, left alone in the tower, were forgotten. Many people believe that Richard III had them murdered so he could become king. In 1674, the bones of two children were discovered buried close to the tower!

You can spend all day at the Tower of London and you still won't see everything. At the Royal Armouries, look for the world's biggest set of armor made for an Indian elephant, along with armor for a giant and a dwarf. And then there's

The tower has always been home to ravens. Legend says that if the ravens disappear, the tower will fall and so will the kingdom. These days, the ravens are brought especially from Scotland, Wales, and the west of England. Their wings are clipped so they can't fly, but ravens only mate in the air! When they die they're buried in a special raven cemetery in the empty moat.

the Jewel House (north of the White Tower) where you can find the Crown Jewels, including the largest cut diamond in the world.

(Mon. to Sat. 9.30–17.00 [5]; Sun. 14.00–17.00 [2–5]. November to February closed Sundays, Mon. to Sat. 9.30–16.00 [4]. Partly accessible for handicapped.)

If you walk out of the Tower of London, you'll find boat docks within 30 feet of the souvenir shop. That's where you can catch a ride down river to Greenwich or the Thames Flood Barriers. (More about that in chap. 8, Rivers and Bridges.)

There's another incredible palace to visit next to the Thames. In 1515, Thomas Wolsey, a very ambitious guy, began building his new house with 1,000 rooms (and 280 silk beds just for guests to sleep over)! It was called **Hampton Court.** Ten years later, he gave it to King Henry VIII (ruler 1509–1547) as a gift. Henry moved into the palace part-time with 1,000 people in the royal household.

Henry remodeled and enlarged the Tudor palace so he'd have more room. Tudor is a style of architecture that was developed during the reign of the Tudor family (1485–1603). You can wander around inside the palace and view the State rooms, the dining room, and the giant kitchen where vast meals were prepared.

In 1689, Christopher Wren made major changes in the Baroque style (which means lots of swirls and ornamentation) for King William III and his Queen Mary who loved the gardens. They planned the "Wilderness" garden where you'll find the famous maze. There's also a restaurant, the Haunted Gallery (where the ghost of Henry's fifth wife, Catherine Howard, is said to wander), and the Cartoon Gallery (the word "cartoon" originally meant a finished sketch for a painting and not Popeye or Superman) with tapestry cartoons by Raphael.

You can also view paintings at Hampton Court by famous artists like Jan Breughel and Jacopo Tintoretto. In the Clock Court, near the center of the palace, look for the astronomical clock that was made especially for King Henry. Notice the earth is the center of the "solar system."

The gardens in Hampton Court are spectacular. Trees are trimmed to resemble giant toadstools, roses bloom in impossible colors, and in the 1800s the famous grapevine produced over 2,000 pounds of grapes per year.

One absolute "must see" is **Hampton Court Maze!** The green hedges, planted and trimmed in a geometrical pattern reaching over your head, make it easy to get lost. Give yourself plenty of time to find the center (you'll know when you get there) because it can take 20 minutes. And then you have to get out! (Hampton Court hours: Daily, 9:30–16.60 [4:30]. Last admission ½-hour before closing. Separate fee for palace and maze. Some facilities for handicapped.) You can quickly and easily travel to Hampton Court by train or bus but allow yourself most of the day for exploring.

If you've ever dreamed of living in an enchanted fairy-tale castle with turrets and towers, then you'll love **Windsor Castle.** William the Conquerer's original wooden castle was a very modest place. But through the years it's been enlarged and rebuilt in stone, until today it seems to fill the sky with golden magic. As you

When you think about knights, Sir Arthur and the Knights of the Round Table might come to mind. The Legend of King Arthur goes back to 6th-century Great Britain. King Arthur was the illegitimate son of King Pendragon. When his father died, he alone could pull the sword, Excalibur, from the stone. Then Merlin, the court magician, told Arthur about his royal parentage. King Arthur and his knights became famous for courage and chivalry.

approach the main gate, stop a moment and imagine the days of knights and chivalry.

During the last 900 years, almost every English ruler has lived in Windsor Castle. Even today the Royal Family stays in residence part of the year, on weekends or holidays. Inside the castle you can view paintings and drawings and a great collection of armor. Outside, on the grounds, there's St. George's Chapel, where King Henry VIII is buried. While you're inside be sure to look up at the spectacular Gothic ceiling.

Don't miss the **Queen's Dollhouse** in Windsor Castle. It might be the world's best dollhouse. It was given to Queen Mary in 1923, and it's a perfect palace within a palace. Electric lights really work, you can lock the doors with keys, and there are even "lifts" to take tiny visitors to other floors. Oh, and the library actually has more than 200 teeny, tiny books especially written for "small" readers. Even though it's a dollhouse, it might be bigger than you are!

If you visit Windsor Castle, it's a good excuse to take a train. You can leave London from Paddington Station. The trip takes about 35 minutes. If you depart from Waterloo Station, it takes a little bit longer to get there, almost 50 minutes.

4. War and Revolution

orld War II was the worst war in history, and it happened barely 50 years ago—during the lives of your grandparents and maybe even your parents. It's important to remember the past, to try and understand what happened, so we comprehend how horrible modern war really is and how much worse nuclear war would be.

Although much of London was destroyed by German bombs, almost all the ruins have disappeared under new buildings and developments. Even so, many older Londoners are veterans of the Second World War and lost friends and family in the carnage. Human lives, unlike buildings, can never be replaced. You can take advantage of your traveling experience to reflect on war and peace.

The **Cabinet War Rooms** lie 17 feet underground. Here you'll find the most important part of the underground emergency accommodation created to protect Winston Churchill, his War Cabinet, and Chiefs of Staff of Britain's armed forces during the brutal air attacks. The nineteen rooms on view include the Cabinet Room, where many of the crucial decisions of World War II were made, the Transatlantic Telephone

Room, where Churchill spoke directly to President Roosevelt in the White House, the Map Room to keep track of all war fronts, and the Prime Minister's Room, where Churchill made his famous wartime broadcasts. The Cabinet War Rooms are maintained to give you a real sense of what it was like to be in the nerve center of the war effort. (Open seven days a week, 10:00–17.50 [5:50]. Last admission 17.15 [5:15]. Clive Steps, King Charles Street. Tel. 01-930 6961 or 01-735 8922. Entry fee.)

Around the corner you can follow Horse Guards Road to the **Horse Guards.** The Guard mounts at 11.00 (10.00 Sundays) daily in ceremonial splendor at Horse Guards Parade in summer and the courtyard in winter.

Political power comes in many shapes and forms. There's official, elected power in the shape of prime ministers like Winston Churchill and Margaret Thatcher. There's another type of power that isn't elected and doesn't have special buildings but throughout time, has changed the course of history—and that's the power of the people. Participating in demonstrations or rallies and casting your vote on election day are just two ways to use people power.

Lots of political rallies have been held in **Trafalgar Square** since the 1820s. Fifty thousand people can gather together at once to let their voices and opinions be heard. It was designed by John Nash (the same person who worked on Buckingham Palace) to celebrate Nelson's victory at Trafalgar. There's a great Christmas tree during the holidays, and you can always hear Big Ben chime clearly. It's also a famous place for pigeons to hang out.

Another "people power" spot is Speaker's Corner in Hyde Park. Sunday morning is the time to find various orators on their soapboxes. (Find out more about it in chap. 6, Parks and Gardens.)

Soldiers are a living reminder of formal power and war. Enter the black and gold gates of the **Royal Hospital,** Chelsea, and you'll see pensioners (retired soldiers) in navy blue uniforms with two rows of buttons and tall, noble hats on their heads. Some of them are very talkative and don't mind questions. One of the best things to see is the fabulous Great Hall where pensioners take tea. There's a colorful mural of Charles II on one wall and the many tables are formally set with small green lamps. You're not allowed to take photographs, so look carefully.

Directly across from the Great Hall, you'll find the Chapel with special pillows set out on the benches. Each pillow has a different insignia for regiments that fought in the war. The Royal

*Inside London is one square mile called the **City of London.** This may sound confusing but the "City" is a strategic center in world financial affairs. At least a third of this area was destroyed by bombs in WW II, but you won't see any evidence because it's all been rebuilt. Barbican Centre, an arts complex completed in 1982, is one of the recent changes. The area of Barbican (in the city) was completely flattened during the WW II Blitz, except for St. Giles Church of Cripplegate. The church still stands in the middle of Barbican Centre, which is the home of the Royal Shakespeare Company (chap. 9, That's Entertainment).*

Engineers have a bright red design with green laurel leaves. In the area outside the Chapel look for the flags taken from different battles displayed on the walls. Outdoors, in the garden green, is a statue of Charles II who laid the foundation stone of the hospital, which was built by Sir Christopher Wren between 1682 and 1692. The Royal Hospital also houses a museum with a collection of almost 2,000 medals, most of which belonged to former in-pensioners.

About 400 in-pensioners live on the grounds. Their rooms are 9 feet by 12 feet and the Royal Hospital is now their home.

(Royal Hospital Road, Great Hall and Chapel hours Mon.–Sat. 10:00–12.00/14.00 [2]–16.00 [4]. Grounds open until 18.00 [6]. Museum 10:00–12.00/14.00–17.00 [5] or until 16.00 in winter. Tel. 01-730 0161. Handicapped access.)

5. Odd and Creepy Things

Ring a-ring a-Rosies
A pocketful of posies,
'Tishoo', 'tishoo',
We all fall down!
This nursery rhyme is
anything but merry. It
dates back to the Great
Plague that raged through
London in 1665. A pink or
"rosie" skin rash signaled
the dreaded plague,
posies were supposed to
protect you, sneezing
('tishoo') meant sure
death, and falling down
was how you died.

hroughout history, London has been the backdrop for lots of life's darker happenings: torture, grave robbing, plague, and witchcraft. Modern London offers you the chance to know about some of the creepier moments of history.

Madame Tussaud (1761–1850) was a very unusual woman. She had a job in Louis XVI's court making wax figures, an art she learned from her uncle. She was sent to prison during the French Revolution, and there she made death masks modeled from the real heads of guillotine victims, including King Louis XVI and Marie Antoinette. In 1802, she took her children and her wax models to England. Finally, she settled in Marylebone when she was 74.

The first thing you'll probably see at **Madame Tussaud's** is a very long line. The summer season is the worst for crowds, but even in winter tourists flock to this famous wax museum. The entry chamber is filled with historical tableaus like the two famous little princes in their royal prison (chap. 3, Rules and Royalty). Most of the faces at Madame Tussaud's are fairly lifelike, but sometimes the hands are even better.

Things get more interesting in the other chambers because you can't tell the crowds of

tourists from the wax. Joan Collins (who doesn't look very real) shares the stage with the Beatles, Michael Jackson, Benjamin Franklin, and John F. Kennedy. But then comes the **Chamber of Horrors.** As you descend the stone staircase, a loud, gloomy bell tolls in your ear. The chamber smells of gunpowder and you're overwhelmed by the sounds of gunshots and the zap of the electric chair. The guillotine is stained with blood, and Madame Tussaud modeled Jean Paul Marat, the French revolutionary, after his murder in the tub when he was still wet from his bath.

Be careful, if you stop to tie your shoelace you could find yourself alone on a deserted and foggy, gaslit street where Jack the Ripper may be hanging out.

(Open daily 10:00–17.30 [5:30]. Tel. 01-935 6861. Entry fee.)

Right next door is the **London Planetarium** and the **Laserium.** You'll see 9,000 stars, moons, and planets created with a Zeiss projector that has 20,000 separate parts. There are daily shows. In the early evening, the same equipment is used along with rock and pop music for a fantastic laser show. If you're really in the mood to spend the day, you can get a combination ticket for Madame Tussaud's, the Planetarium, and Laserium.

(Open daily 11:00–16.30 [4:30]. Tel. 01-486 1121. If you need assistance for handicapped, ring in advance for Madame Tussaud's, the Planetarium, and the Laserium. Ring Laserline for show information, 01-486 2242.)

Walk down Marylebone Street from Madame Tussaud's, turn the corner, and you're on Baker Street where Sherlock Holmes lived in the fiction of Sir Arthur Conan Doyle. Holmes's

address, 221B Baker Street, really exists since the street was renumbered in 1930. But you definitely have to sleuth out the reminders of the gas lamps and hansom cabs that existed in his day.

Another haven for aficionados of the creepy is the **London Dungeon,** located in the vaults beneath London Bridge Station, where you can return to the days of torture, witchcraft, and disease, including the smells, sights, and sounds. Life-size exhibits feature almost every disgusting aspect of British medieval history. There's also a newly opened exhibit of Pudding Lane where the Great Fire of London started on September 1, 1666. Special effects with light and sound add to the chills and thrills, but the dungeon is not for unaccompanied kids or those with queasy stomachs, and people under ten should think twice before going in because it's pretty scary.

(The London Dungeon is located at 28/34 Tooley Street, tel. 01-403 0606. Take the London Bridge tube. Open daily 10:00–16.30 [4:30]. Some handicapped access. Telephone in advance for assistance.)

Another Tooley Street attraction is **Space Adventure** featuring Starship 3001. This is a computer-simulated experience where you're launched into the sights and sounds of deep-space travel. Your mission is to rescue a stranded airship near the red planet, Mars, but huge meteor showers threaten to smash you to smithereens! If the outer limits give you an appetite, there's a snack shop offering spacey treats like Pulsar Pizzas and Black Hole Gateau.

(Located at 64-66 Tooley St., Space Adventure is open May to Oct. 10:30–18.00 [6] weekdays and 10:00–18.00 weekends. All other months,

Space Adventure, Tooley Street

it is open 10:30-17.00[5]. Tel. 01-378 1405.)

Sometimes the best place for a scare is a good, old-fashioned cemetery. **Highgate Cemetery** is one of the best. If you go to Highgate, make sure to enter the famous Egyptian Gates and wander up Egyptian Avenue (it looks like a mummy will appear any minute). When you reach the Catacombs you might be able to peer through a crack in the mossy stones into the underground tombs. And look on top of the Circle of Lebanon for the amazing cyprus tree that spreads its branches over the circular-patterned tombs.

Now that it's a nature reserve and protected by a registered charity, you can't wander around by yourself, but maybe that's for the best. Highgate Cemetery is home to 170,000 bodies!

The western portion of Highgate Cemetery was opened by the London Cemetery Company in 1839 because London's church graveyards were full. In 1854, the Eastern Cemetery was

London has more than its share of haunted houses. Hampton Court has the haunted gallery where two wives of Henry VIII have been seen wandering around like ghosts do. Jane Seymour, who died in childbirth, carries around a candle and moans sadly. Catherine Howard, who eventually had her head chopped off, is said to rush around trying to find her husband (the king) and plead her case. Elephant and Castle tube station is known for strange clankings and footsteps. The British Museum, renowned for mummies dating back to 4500 B.C., also boasts a ghost who, naturally, dresses up as an Egyptian princess. Another ghost who used to be a Victorian actor, but was murdered, still performs by haunting Covent Garden tube station and the Adelphi Theatre where he worked.

opened and the fashionable society of Victorian London used to stroll past the numerous tombs, vaults, and monuments on Sunday afternoons. It was the place to see and be seen.

(Guided tours are led through Western Highgate. Hours are subject to change, but you can probably find a tour on the hour from 10:00–16.00 [4] on weekends and at 12.00, 14.00 [2], and 16.00 [4], on weekdays.)

The Northern Line of the tube stops at Archway and from there you can walk up Highgate Hill, cross through Waterlow Park and stop for tea, and continue your walk (5–10 minutes) to the cemetery. Hampstead Heath is also in the same neighborhood (chap. 6, Parks and Gardens).

There are two sides to the cemetery, the Western Cemetery, where writer Charles Dickens's wife, Catherine, and 8-month-old daughter, Dora, are buried, and the Eastern Cemetery, where you'll find both tomb and monument for Karl Marx, the socialist philosopher who wrote Das Kapital.

There's also the **Horniman Museum** (100 London Rd., tel. 01-699 2339, admission free) with a Cult of the Dead section (Osiris was the Egyptian king of the dead, and special rituals were described in the Book of the Dead), mummies, and an ancient Egyptian tomb.

Piccadilly Circus, Soho, is NOT a circus! It's where Piccadilly Street and Regent Street intersect. In the old days, they converged in a circular pattern.

At the end of the eighteenth century, there was a scandal over grave robbers who dug up corpses and sold them to doctors for medical research.

The Trocadero, on Shaftesbury Avenue and Coventry Street, offers modern mall conveniences: shopping, eating, and entertainment. That's where you'll find **The Guinness World of Records,** two floors of life-size exhibits featuring the world's fattest, tallest, shortest, and some of the weirdest! Plastic models show off Arnold Schwarzenegger's "best body" along with nature's biggest vegetables. One of GWR's highlights is a scale with the fattest man on one side. Kids get together and climb on the other side to see how many of them it takes to balance the weight.

6. Parks and Gardens

Parks are inexpensive, democratic, and often surprising places to spend a lazy afternoon or even an entire day.

If you stepped into a time machine and zipped back to 1637, you'd find people strolling around **Hyde Park** almost like they do today. For the past 300 years, it has been the scene of horse races, duels, and royal hunts. Hyde Park encompasses over 300 acres of grass, trees, gardens, and even a lake.

But **Speaker's Corner,** near Marble Arch, has only been around since 1872 when the government okayed this unassuming spot for free speech and public debate. You'll find men and

women of all shapes, sizes, and colors standing on soapboxes and preaching eloquently to the interested crowds. The subject could be anything, but religion is especially popular, and spectators join in whenever they feel bold enough. Spend some time at Speaker's Corner because it's a good time to think about the great privilege of free speech!

An easy stroll through Hyde Park takes you past equestrians, men playing soccer, people lounging in folding chairs, and babies in strollers to **The Serpentine,** a small lake where you can rent a rowboat or a paddleboat, take a dip (brrrrr), or feed the waterfowl for free.

It's difficult to tell where Hyde Park ends and **Kensington Gardens** begins. It doesn't really matter because they're both green and lovely and together they cover 600 acres. But the tail end of The Serpentine lake becomes **The Long Water** (a narrow curve of water) and then you're in the gardens. You'll find the famous statue of **Peter Pan** (by Sir G. Frampton, 1912) at the edge of The

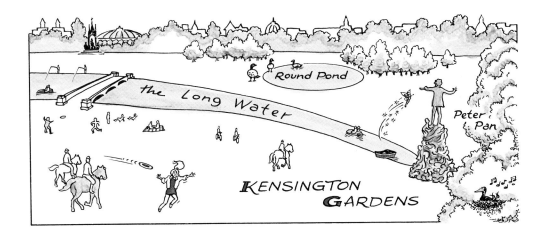

Long Water where he first landed his boat in the fairy play. Take some time to examine all the delightful details in the base of the sculpture. Then you might continue west toward the Children's Playground and the Elfin Oak where finger-sized, colorful elves romp and play in the old oak trunk.

Regent's Park is one of the biggest in central London. There are rose gardens, boats to hire, and plenty of room for sports like cricket, football, and lacrosse. And during the summer you may happen upon music or entertainment in the open-air theater.

If you love animals and find safety in numbers, the **London Zoo** (in Regent's Park) is home to 8,000 creatures. The zoo dates back to 1826, and some major renovations are taking place. Favorites include the giant panda, lions, tigers, and the Reptile House filled with alligators and snakes. The miracle of technology and reversed lighting has created Moonlight World, where spiny anteaters, bats, and kiwis do their stuff in

At Kensington Gardens, try to spot the elves at the Elfin Oak.

At Kew Garden, visit the Great Pagoda for a taste of China.

the "dark of night" while you watch in daylight! Specials include feeding time, camel and llama rides, and live shows daily. There's also the Zoo Waterbus, one of the best ways to see exotic zoo creatures from April to September.

(Open 9:00–18.00 [6] summer. Sun. 9:00–19.00 [7]. Winter 10.00–dusk. Tel. 01-722 3333.)

You can wander through almost 300 acres of exotic plants, trees, and flowers at **Kew Gardens.** These Royal Botanical Gardens grew from humble beginnings (7 acres) before Princess Augusta decided to enlarge things in the mid-1700s. Plant houses include the refrigerated Alpine House, Australian House, and Tropical Waterlily House where you'll be dwarfed by giant lily pads. Leave yourself lots of time to explore the gardens outside where you'll find azaleas, Japanese cherries, a bamboo garden, and some very rare plant species. The Royal Residence, **Kew Palace,** near the main gates (open Apr. to Sept., daily 11:00–17.30 [5:30]), was built by Samuel Fortrey in the early 1600s. It's also known as the Dutch House, not because he got in trouble but because his ancestors came from Holland. Behind Kew Palace, you'll find a small kitchen garden. Queen Charlotte, who raised her children in the royal residences, designed a quaint picnic cottage called (not surprisingly) the **Queen's Cottage** (1772). Upstairs you'll find tea for two set out invitingly —but before you sit down, remember, it's a museum. You can find your own refreshments at the pavilion.

(Kew Gardens is open year-round. Come early, at least two hours before closing, because you need lots of time. Daily 10:00–16.00 [4] winter, 10:00–20.00 [8] summer (closed Good Friday and

Dec. 24, 25, 26). Tel. 01-940 1171. Entry fee.)

Hampstead Heath is another very big park (800 acres). If you find a high spot like Parliament Hill (319 feet above sea level), you'll have a nice view of London. It's also a terrific place to fly kites summer or winter.

The heath wasn't always a park (maids from nearby fancy houses used to lay the laundry out to dry here), but it's been a place to relax and have fun for a very long time. It's terrific for bird-watchers so bring your binoculars. And don't forget a swimming suit; even in winter, very brave folks go out to crack the ice on the ponds before they dip in. If you happen to have a fishing rod handy, you can cast out in the pond nearest Parliament Hill.

Hampstead Heath is close to Highgate Cemetery (chap. 5, Odd and Creepy Things). To get there you can take the tube to the Hampstead station and then catch a bus. Ask for directions at the tube station.

In the twelfth century, boys (these were the days before the Equal Rights Amendment!) invented ice skates by strapping animal bones to their feet with leather thongs and skating over London's frozen marshes.

Knights and kings and castles were a vibrant part of England's medieval life and legend. So a young man was likely to spend his Sunday afternoons in the fields around London, practicing the skills of war—with shield and sword, bow and quiver.

Battersea Park, across the Thames from Chelsea, is 200 acres of wide open fun. It's a great place to find special events like fairs, open-air concerts, and dancing. If you run out of energy, you can buy snacks near the boating lake, and for younger brothers and sisters, there's a children's zoo.

(Battersea Arts Centre is mostly accessible for handicapped, telephone in advance. Tel. 01-223 8413.)

The gardens at **Hampton Court** (chap. 3, Rules and Royalty) are sensational: roses, rare plants, and formal courtyards with charming fountains. When the gardeners are working, you may find smelly piles of manure and compost here and there. Look at how dark the earth is. And, of course, take time to explore **Hampton Court Maze**.

The town of Greenwich is filled with picturesque buildings, winding streets, and pretty gardens. It sits right on the edge of the Thames and the shops, restaurants, and museums surround **Greenwich Park.**

It's a 20-minute walk from the National Maritime Museum (chap. 7, Museums) through the park to the top of the hill and the Old Royal Observatory. But you can make it in 5 minutes if you run all the way! Whether you walk or run, make sure you arrive at the Old Royal Observatory by 13.00 hours so you can set your watch by the falling Timeball. Then stand astride the brass Meridian Zero. Greenwich was selected in 1884 as the prime or zero meridian. All other North/South longitudinal lines are measured from the Greenwich meridian. Do you know the longitude where you live?

7. Museums

he world is full of fabulous creations and London's museums hold more than their fair share.

Not too far from Hyde Park you could spend days viewing and participating in some of the great discoveries of humankind. The **Science Museum** offers a mind-boggling array of exhibits. Choose from oil, steam, wind, and turbine engines (Galleries Two and Three), exploration in space and the Apollo 10 capsule (Gallery Six), or the oldest locomotive in the world. If your parents came to the Science Museum when they were your age, they probably remember the Children's Gallery on the lower ground floor. There are exhibits of toys and things, but nothing to DO because things have changed a lot since those days. So give yourself plenty of time for the Launch Pad upstairs.

Recently relocated, the **Launch Pad** offers three sections where you can interact with displays. The test bed area has newer, more experimental exhibits. The regular area has tried-and-true favorites like the grain loader where you can climb aboard and send buckets of wheat along the loading belt for grinding and processing. You can hold up something that

When you visit the
Launch Pad, have a
shocking experience!

looks like a ray gun and color your own video image on a TV screen. The darkroom guarantees sparks with glowing globes, electric rays, and heat sensors.

(To avoid crowds, it's best to come weekdays after 16.00 [4]; admission free from 16.30 [4:30]–17.40 [5:40]. Kids under 13 need to be with someone over 18. Hours are 10:30–17.40 [5:40], except Sundays 11:00–17.40 [5:40]. Tel. 01-589 3456. Some handicapped access, telephone in advance.)

You don't even have to come up for air to find the **Natural History Museum.** It's an easy walk below ground level through the Centre Hall with all the locomotives.

Diplodocus carnegii stands proudly, all 26 meters of him, in the spectacular central hall of the **Natural History Museum.** He's a plaster cast of the original dinosaur skeleton (from Wyoming) dating back 150 million years. Before you leave the main hall, look for the stone monkeys climbing the corners of the room.

Popular exhibits include Discovering Mammals, with a life-size model of a blue whale, and Human Biology (find out how your body works), with interactive computer technology. If you're visiting during British school holidays (August and 2 weeks of Easter), head for the Discovery Center. Past exhibits included a chick hatchery, a giant model of a mole tunnel with a humongous worm, and a display of hundreds of live butterflies!

(Hours 10:00–18.00 [6], except Sunday 13.00 [1]–18.00 [6]. Closed Christmas Eve, Christmas Day, Boxing Day, New Year's Day, Good Friday, and May Day. Tel. 01-725 7866. Entry fee. Some handicapped access, telephone in advance.)

The **Geological Museum** is housed in the same complex. The incredible story of the Earth is on view with rare rock specimens, relief models, photographs, and maps. For those who love shiny and expensive things, there's the world-famous gemstone collection—diamonds, emeralds, sapphires, and rubies.

(Some handicapped access, telephone in advance. Tel. 01-938 8765. Entry fee.)

The **Victoria and Albert Museum** next door features displays of early medieval art, musical instruments, and treasures from the Far East. Best to see are the completely furnished rooms from different periods of history like the eighteenth-century music room, a Gothic room (remember chap. 3, Rules and Royalty?) and a room from a seventeenth-century inn.

Visit Diplodocus carnegii *in the central hall of the Natural History Museum.*

If you're a movie buff, there's a great new spot for lights, camera, action! MOMI, the **Museum of Moving Image,** offers more than fifty exhibits where you can participate to your heart's content. Why not try your hand at editing? Or anchor the news at 10. Or give an interview to Barry Norman, London's famous weekly TV and film critic. A videotape of Norman asks you questions, you answer for real, and technicians put you together on the spot. Presto, instant interview.

MOMI is staffed with actors, actresses, and technicians ready to answer questions. For a flash from the past you can visit a real "picture house" from the 1930s. An usherette escorts you to your seat spouting local cockney chat to courting couples and popcorn addicts; this even predates your parents! If you're an animation freak, you can study the eighteenth- and nineteenth-century animation machines and make your own cartoons. Just draw your own character on a strip of paper, put paper inside the Zoetrope (animation machine), spin it, and watch the action. Word has it you should plan to spend all day at MOMI, but take a lunch. In the future, there may be food facilities, but for now your stomach will be growling long before you're ready to leave.

(South Bank. Waterloo tube station. Admission fee. Tues. through Sat. 10:00–20.00 [8], Sun. 10:00–18.00 [6] A 24-hour hotline gives information: 01-401 2636. Handicapped access, telephone in advance. Tel. 01-928 3232.)

At the **British Museum,** the mummies are not to be missed. Then there's the Rosetta stone covered with ancient hieroglyphics and the

If you've always wanted to fly, at MOMI, you can lie on a slanted board and whizz over the rooftops of London. The secret is the blue background that even Superman uses in real movies.

Elgin marbles, from the Acropolis in Athens, Greece, dating back to the 4th century B.C. The marbles are controversial because Thomas Bruce, 7th Earl of Elgin, spent time in Greece and collected many works of art that were in danger of being destroyed. In 1816, he sold the Elgin marbles to the British government (for half what they cost him) and now many people believe they should be given back to the Greeks because they're part of Greek history and culture. That's something to think about while you explore the British Museum.

The museum is full of the wonders of the world. Another incredible place to view is the Reading Room in the museum. You have to talk to the guards before you can go in. Sometimes there's a short wait before you're guided inside for a look. Scholars use this library to research their books.

(Great Russell Street. Open Mon.–Sat. 10:00–17.00 [5], Sun 14.30 [2:30]–18.00 [6]. Admission free. Tel. 01-636 1555. Handicapped access, telephone in advance.)

For ships, the ocean, and naval history, nothing beats the **National Maritime Museum** in

Outside the National Maritime Museum, you'll find the dolphin sundial where time is told to the minute by shadowy dolphin tails.

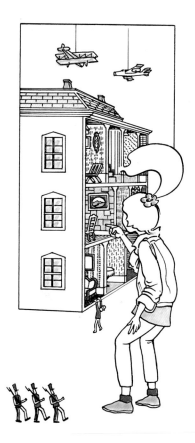

*London is loaded with beautiful toys. **Pollock's Toy Museum** will knock your socks off if you're into dollhouses, tin soldiers, board games, or Victorian toy theaters.*

(1 Scala St. Tel. 01-636 3452. Mon.–Sat. 10:00–17.00 [5].)

Greenwich Park (chap. 6, Parks and Gardens). The museum is impressive on the outside and fascinating on the inside. You enter the grounds through the beautiful black and gold Royal Gates. Museum buildings include the glorious Queen's House, designed by Inigo Jones (a famous English architect). Inside the museum, actual boats, ship models, maritime artifacts, and memorabilia are displayed. You can learn about Lord Nelson (1758–1805; he defeated the French and Spanish fleets at Trafalgar but was mortally wounded), Sir Francis Drake (1540–1596; the first Englishman to circumnavigate the world), and Captain James Cook (1728-1779; he explored Australia and New Zealand and sailed around the world).

Neptune Hall, West Wing, boasts the world's largest ship in a bottle along with the history of the boat, from prehistory to modern times. You can also see *Reliant*, a paddle tug built in 1907. After a life cruising up and down the Manchester Ship Canal, she was restored and welded together inside Neptune Hall. Now she's in complete working order, engines and all. Ooh and aah over Victorian pleasure boats or the triple-expansion steam engine. The Barge House offers time to explore Prince Frederick's barge, dating to 1732, gilded and elegant. The barge was used by the Royal Family for more than 100 years.

(Romney Road. Mon.–Sat. 10:00–18.00 [6] and Sunday 14.00 [2]–18.00 [6]. In winter, closed 17.00 [5] every day. Admission includes the Old Royal Observatory and the Meridian, which is at the top of Greenwich Park Hill [chap. 6, Parks and Gardens]. Some handicapped access, telephone in advance. Tel. 01-858 4422.)

London Transport Museum is tucked into the heart of Covent Garden. Packed with trains, buses, trams, and trolleys, the museum offers a vast view of London's public transport history. And the working exhibits will keep you busy. Try yourself out as a signalperson. Flip a switch and watch an early model of an underground lift go into action. And discover what happens when you pull "dead man's handle" on a tube train.

(10:00–18.00 [6] every day, except Dec. 24, 25, 26. Admission fee. Some handicapped access [and free admission], telephone in advance. Tel. 01-379 6344.)

Dickens's House is a different kind of museum. You'll find lots of the author's memorabilia, portraits, and letters. And the rooms are much like they were when Charles Dickens lived there and created characters like Oliver Twist and Scrooge.

(48 Doughty Street. Mon.–Sat. 9:30–17.00 [5]. Admission fee.)

For a look inside Victorian shops or a cell from Newgate Prison, try the **Museum of London,** just a five-minute walk from either St. Paul's or Barbican tube station. The museum is off street level so you go up the steps to a high walkway. There's a room for every period of the history of London. The Roman room includes leather shoes, clothes, and artifacts. There's also a model of the Great Fire of London (1666) that lights up for a miniature reenactment of the fire.

(Barbican, The City. Tues.–Sat. 10:00–18.00 [6]. Sun. 14.00 [2]–18.00. Tel. 01-600 3699. Free admission. Wheelchairs available, telephone in advance.)

London Toy & Model Museum boasts mechanical toys, tin toys, trains, and other toys that don't start with T.

(23 Craven Hill. Tel. 01-262 7905. Tues.–Sat. 10:00–17.30 [5:30]. Sun. 11:00–17.00 [5]. Some handicapped access.)

Bethnal Green Museum of Childhood has spectacular Russian dolls, rocking horses, and miniature engines on view. For theater fans, there's an authentic Punch and Judy booth.

(Handicapped access. Cambridge Heath Road. Tel. 01-980 2415. Mon.– Thurs., Sat. 10:00–18.00 [6]. Sun. 14.30 [2:30]–18.00.)

8. Rivers and Bridges

T he Roman ruler, Caesar, called the great river Tamesis and had a wooden bridge built across it. Today, the river is called the Thames, and getting on the river is a fun way to see some of London's best sights like the Tower Bridge and the Thames Flood Barrier along with lots of flotsam and jetsam. You can take tour boats (for reasonable fees) up and down the river from Westminster Pier, Charing Cross Pier, the Tower Pier, and Greenwich Pier.

Next to the Tower of London, **The Tower Bridge** opens up its roadway a half dozen times a week when boats give the signal. Now you can tour inside the bridge. There's the Engine Room Museum, glassed-in overhead walkways, and a massive Victorian steam engine (still pumping) installed nearly 100 years ago to raise and lower the gates.

(The bridge is an easy walk from Tower Hill Underground. Open 7 days a week at 10.00. Last visitor 17.45 [5:45] or 16.00 [4]. Nov. 1–Mar. 31.)

If you're looking for the "Centre of the World," try the borough of **Greenwich** where you can stand on the zero meridian line (chap. 6, Parks and Gardens). You can easily spend a whole day

What is London Bridge doing in Lake Havasu, Arizona? The first London Bridge, built by the Romans, was rebuilt many times. Eventually, still another, bigger bridge was needed so the old bridge was sold to Lake Havasu for one million pounds.

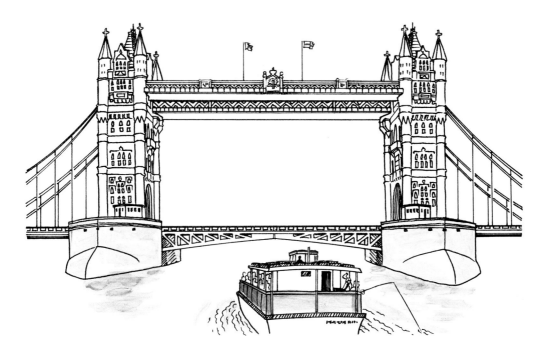

with plenty of fascinating things to see along with shopping and eating and just plain meandering on the beautiful streets.

If you get to Greenwich by riverboat, the first thing you can do is climb aboard the dry-docked *Cutty Sark Clipper*. Built in 1869, she's a beautiful 280-foot Tea Clipper fully rigged for harbor. On open sea her fastest speed was 17 knots (one knot = 1.15 mph). (Greenwich Pier. Mon.–Sat. 10:00–18.00 [6] and Sun. 12:00–18.00, 17.00 [5] in winter, 7 days a week. Admission fee. Some handicapped access.)

Cutty Sark's neighbor is the *Gypsy Moth*, famous for a solo round-the-world voyage when the late Sir Francis Chichester raced her 29,677 miles and 226 days at sea. (Open to the public March to end of October.)

Now that you've been on the river, try walking

River pirates, scuffle hunters, and other thieves cruised the Thames in early days. If you sail along the river past Wapping, look for the Town of Ramsgate, a pub dating from the 1600s. After a nearby trial with a very strict judge, pirates were tied to the pub's pier at low tide. There they stayed for punishment until the waters rose and fell three times. Another historical spot in Wapping is Execution Dock, where Captain Kidd and various other pirates were hanged.

Down below deck on the Cutty Sark, *you can drop 10 pence in the coin slot and hear recorded historical tidbits or check out the amazing collection of ship's figureheads (the carved and painted wooden figures that decorate the ship's bow).*

under it. The **Greenwich Foot Tunnel** connects Greenwich to Isle of the Dogs, which Henry VIII used as a hunting ground (and where he kept his royal dogs). On the Greenwich side, you'll enter the tunnel from a small domed building in Cutty Sark Gardens. Proceed through the drippy tunnel and don't think about all the water pressure surrounding you. On Isle of the Dogs, you'll come out in Island Gardens, a small park. The isle became the center of the London dockyards in the early 1800s. Now it's part of a redevelopment plan informally known as yuppification. From the park, you can easily stroll to Island Garden Station where the elevated **Docklands Light Railway** stops every 10 minutes. Hop aboard with your camera because this train gives you an overhead view of London's docks, a bit of the ruin and rubble from WW II, and the city of Charles Dickens's famous books. (Small fee.) From Island Gardens, it's a good view back to Greenwich. And now you have to walk all the way back, but it's only a bit longer than the width of the river.

From Greenwich you can catch a boat downriver to the **Thames Flood Barrier**, which has saved London several times.

London is sinking at a rate of 12 inches every century. The lower it goes, the more likely the Thames will flood the city. Three hundred people died in 1953 from flooding. The flood barrier, completed in 1983, was constructed so this would never happen again. Seven thousand drawings were needed for planning. During construction, 250 divers worked in zero visibility water. The barrier, with ten steel gates, reaches 520 meters from shore to shore. The four main gates each weigh 3,700 tons, and there's a 30-minute maximum closure time. It's best to see the barrier from the river. Then you can go ashore to the Thames Barrier Visitors Centre and see a video, an audiovisual show, and a working model.

(Small entry fee. Mon.–Fri. 10:30–17.00 [5]. Sat.–Sun. 10:30–17.30 [5:30]. Tel. 01-854 1373. Handicapped access. If you decide to take the train instead of the boat, the Charlton Train Station is 15 minutes walk from the Visitors Centre.)

Trading ships traveled on the Thames to and from the open sea. Often, on stormy nights, ships were overdue. The **Lutine Bell** was rung twice if the ship was safe and only once if she was wrecked. The bell is on view at the futuristic Lloyd's of London building, designed by Richard Rogers. (Lime St., tel. 01-623 7100. Mon.–Fri. 10:00–16:00 [4].)

Riverboat Information Services for London Tourist Board: 730 4812. A recorded voice gives you information and referral numbers for cruises to and from Westminster Pier, Charing Cross Pier, the Tower Pier, Greenwich Pier, and the Thames Flood Barrier.

From afar, the Thames Flood Barrier looks like a series of giant metal monsters, heads raised and eyes blinking green and red. Close up, they take on an eerie beauty.

9. That's Entertainment

J ugglers, actors, writers, magicians! London past and present is filled with entertainment. Theaters abound, some dating back hundreds of years. There's the Haymarket, Prince of Wales, Adelphi, and Her Majesty's, just to name a few. With at least fifty major theaters to choose from, you can see shows like "The Phantom of the Opera," "Starlight Express," "Me and My Girl," and of course the longest-running show in the world, "The Mousetrap." London is pure heaven for thespians.

Covent Garden, named for the monks of Westminster Abbey who kept a garden in the Middle Ages, has a rowdy and theatrical reputation. In the 1700s it was known for bawdy houses, pickpockets, and a theater monopoly. Today it's still famous for footlights and greasepaint.

One of Covent Garden's oldest theaters is **Theatre Royal, Drury Lane,** opened in 1663 and frequented by King Charles II. There he watched many an evening's entertainment and fell in love with the actress, Nell Gwynne.

The **Royal Opera House** on Bow Street is just plain beautiful with a creamy white and gold auditorium, a proscenium decorated by Raffaelle

Pick up a weekly copy of Early Times—Independent Newspaper for Young People *as soon as you arrive in London. Written for kids, by kids, it gives you the latest in world news, cartoons, political interviews, and entertainment reviews.*

Monti, and a romantic foyer. If you get a chance, go inside.

St. Paul's Church, near the Piazza, is known as the actor's church. The walls are covered with memorials to actors, actresses, and artists. This is where Samuel Pepys saw the first recorded performance of a Punch and Judy show in 1662. A plaque marks the spot.

Street entertainment continues (around Covent Garden Market) today with mimes, magicians, and assorted show-biz folks doing their thing. Inside Covent Garden Central Market musicians play everything from folk to funky. Another tradition—pickpockets—continues, so keep an eye on your wallet.

The idea of a national theater was around for a long time in London. But only in 1962 did it become official with Lawrence Olivier, the famous actor, in charge. More than ten years later, the new complex across the Thames was finally ready. The **National Theatre,** at Southbank, includes three theaters: the Olivier, the Lyttleton, and the Cottesloe. It's a fabulous opportunity to see anything theatrical, from the classics to the most avant-garde. But you must book seats as soon as you can. (Tel. 01-928 2252.)

When earls and lords rode to the hounds, the hunting cry was "So-ho!" And that's probably how **Soho,** the area of London directly west of Covent Garden, got its name. In the seventeenth century, it was a fashionable place to live. Then it became the spot where immigrants decided to settle. When the poor move into areas, the rich often sell their houses and leave. In the 1800s, that's what happened, and Soho developed a reputation for music halls, writers, and eccen-

Backstage is almost more fun than center stage! Two theaters offer tours behind the scenes: **National Theatre** *(South Bank, tel. 01-633 0880) and* **Barbican Centre,** *where the Royal Shakespeare Company is in residence (Silk St., tel. 01-638 4141; handicapped access).*

trics. In the early twentieth century, Soho became known as a fashionable "dining area." You can still find great food and nightlife in Soho, but some of the entertainment is definitely adult.

Ask your parents about Chelsea in the 1960s. **King's Road** used to be exactly that a long time ago—a private road for kings. Then, in the 60s, along with the Beatles, it became famous for street entertainment, girls in miniskirts, and long-haired boys in paisley shirts. In the late 70s, punk became fashionable enough for postcards and you can still spot some green and purple mohawks cruising the neighborhoods. But mostly Chelsea is a quiet and pretty residential area nowadays.

10. Shopping

The exchange rate fluctuates in London just like in the rest of the world. When you arrive, you should check at the banks or money exchange for exact rates.

hopping can be one of the pleasures of traveling. What you find in a city's stores tells you a lot about it's people. London has some very special stores with novel gifts for friends back home. And even if you're on a budget, you can always afford to window shop.

At **Harrod's,** on Brompton Road, there are some odd things to buy, like a toy caterpillar that's 250 feet long and costs almost $6,000. It's a department store but it looks like a palace. Even the Queen of England shops there. Make sure you find the food halls on the ground floor. There's meat, cheese, and sweets, too. But the best of all is the fish hall where men in aprons carve sculptures every day out of colorful fresh fish. Fish never looked so good! Don't forget, Harrod's toy department is a good place to hang out while your parents look at English silver.

If you want to shop some more, **Hamley's** on Regent Street could be the best place in the world for toys, toys, and more toys. If you check out the Leggo Department, you may find Buckingham Palace and life-size Beefeaters made out of Leggo! But you'll also find every kind of action toy imaginable and some you'd never dream of.

A different kind of store in another part of

town is **Fortnum & Mason's,** no. 181 Piccadilly. One of the best things about F&M is keeping track of time. When the famous clock strikes the hour, almost life-size statues of Mr. Fortnum and Mr. Mason glide out of their kiosks and bow to each other. All the while 17 bells play old-fashioned tunes and Mr. F and Mr. M bow again and then disappear inside their kiosks.

Grown-ups think you can't go to London without tasting English tea with scones and jam, and they're probably right! The restaurant on the ground floor of F&M is best for that kind of stuff. But if you have a real sweet tooth, there's a whole department just for chocolate where clerks (pronounced "clarks") wear special uniforms that look pretty silly. You can even buy a canned boar's head if you need one.

Burlington Arcade, near the Royal Academy and Old Bond Street, dates back to 1819, and the storefronts look it. Before you make a spectacle of yourself, read the signs that warn no whistles or screams lest the beadles (uniformed attendants) get you!

Portobello Market, on Portobello Road, offers strolling shoppers blocks and blocks of things to buy, everything from pricey antiques to flea-market items.

(The market is closed on Thursday, and Saturday is the big market day. Portobello Road is an easy walk from Nottinghill tube station.)

11. The Sporting Life

London isn't London without sports! For a really peculiar and interesting pastime, try **cricket,** the English national game. Cricket games can last 5 days before a win, lose, or draw. But if you venture out to the **Lord's Cricket Ground** on a Sunday afternoon, you're guaranteed about 4 hours of fun and a probable win or lose. The rules and protocol are puzzling, but you can always find a courteous Londoner in the stands who will explain the basics. You'll find historical highlights and mementos in the Cricket Memorial Gallery on the grounds, but it's only open during the games. For more informal cricket, there are impromptu games during the summer at any recreation ground. (Lord's Cricket Ground, St. John's Wood. Tel. 01-289 1616.)

Soccer is probably played more often than any other game on the planet. In London (and most of the world) soccer is called **football.** It's not the same as American football, but it's no different in one respect: people get very emotional about their team. Most stadiums have family cages (screened-in areas) just in case fans get too rowdy. Some of London's teams are the Queen's Park Rangers and the Tottenham Hotspurs (who play at White Hart Lane stadium), also known as the

"Spurs" by fans. Division games are played every week until May and then the FA (Football Association) Cup is played at Wembley Stadium. Just think of it as London's Superbowl!

Rugby football (also called rugger) is more like American football than soccer. Getting confused? Oh well, there are lots of Rugby Clubs where amateur games are played on weekends. The big professional playoffs include England vs. Scotland and France in the odd years and England vs. Wales and Ireland in the even years. That happens in January at Twickenham Stadium, another Superbowl, this one for rugger fans.

Of course, every spring there's some of the world's best tennis to be seen at Wimbledon. And Epsom Downs offers a chance to enjoy a very English tradition, steeplechase and flat course horse races and the Derby in June.

12. Getting Around Town

Once in London you'll probably do lots of walking, but you have three main choices for public transportation: taxi, bus, or subway.

Before you go anywhere, purchase a copy of ***AZ London*** Street Atlas (A to Zed)! It's the standard London map book covering central London and the suburbs. You'll see Londoners carrying AZ under their arms. The back cover has the official underground (subway or tube) map that you'll probably be using all the time.

English **taxis** are different from American taxis. There's more legroom and they look very dignified. And, of course, the driver sits on the *right* side of the cab. But just like with New York cabs, if it's raining you'll never find one. If you're in a new part of town, ask people where you should stand. People usually queue up and look for a taxi with its flag up or a for-hire sign.

The **buses** come in two layers: single-deckers and the picturesque double-deckers. If the bus is a front loader, you pay the driver exact fare as you climb aboard. If it's a bus with automatic doors at the tail-end, just jump on and a conductor will be round to collect fares and hand out tickets. But watch out because London bus routes are confusing, and the drivers are either very nice or very grumpy!

The **Underground** is also called the **Tube.** It's a cheap and easy way to get about London. Many platforms have electric signs with train destinations listed. And there are easy maps of all the tube lines at every stop.

If you want to go out of town, **trains** are the way to travel. Train stations are right next to the tube stations. Oh, and don't forget to tell your little brother or sister that Paddington Bear got left behind in Paddington Train Station.

London Transport offers all sorts of deals. You can get special cards good for tubes, trains, and buses in Greater London and you can "swan" around all day, as they say. There are other bargains if you just ask.

When you need information on London's buses or underground, call 222-1234, 24 hours a day. That's the number of London Transport's **Travel Information Services.** There are offices at Victoria, Piccadilly Circus, King's Cross, Euston, Oxford Circus, St. James's Park, and Heathrow.

For river transportation, call London Tourist Board, **Riverboat Information Services** at 01-730 4812.

Remember that traffic moves on opposite sides of the street in England. The roads are painted with reminders to "look left" or "look right." It's scary at first, so BE CAREFUL when you're crossing streets.

Glossary

How to Speak English

People in London speak English, supposedly. . . But it probably doesn't sound like any English you've heard before. If you try and fit a "bonnet" on your head, you're guaranteed a big headache. And be careful not to drop your "iced lollie" in the "loo" or go outside without your "brolly"! If all that sounds like Greek to you, just take a peek at the Glossary.

British	American
Tube, underground	Subway
Queue	Line (of people)
Pavement	Sidewalk
Iced lollie	Popsicle
Knickers	Underpants
Hooter	Car horn
Biscuits	Cookies
Sweets	Candy
Gents or Ladies	Public rest room
Loo	Bathroom (in a private home)
Fortnight	Two weeks
Brolly	Umbrella
On holiday	Vacation
Boot	Trunk (of car)
Trousers	Pants
Tart	Pie

British	American
Ironmonger	Hardware store
Chemist	Drugstore
Engaged tone	Busy signal (on telephone)
Petrol	Gasoline
Bonnet	Hood (of car)
Crackers	Fireworks
Lorry	Truck
Tip lorry	Dump truck
Dust bin	Garbage can
Torch	Flashlight
Nappies	Diapers
Lift	Elevator
Single ticket	One-way ticket
Ground floor	First floor
Mate	Friend
Grotty	Dirty
Cheers	Thanks, good-bye
Ta	Thanks
Zed	"Z" (the letter)
Crisps	Potato chips
Chips	Fries
Tomato catsup	Ketchup
Quid, Nicker	Pound (English money)
Five "P"	Five pence (English money)
Flat	Apartment
Newsagent	Stand or shop where magazines and newspapers are sold

Calendar of Events

January
Rugby: Triple Crown and International Championship at Twickenham Royal Epiphany at Chapel Royal, St James's Palace
Wreath laying at the statue of Charles I, Trafalgar Square, Banqueting Hall
Chinese New Year procession, Soho

February
Cruft's Dog Show, Earls Court
Blessing of Throats, St. Ethelreda, Ely Place
English Folk Dance and Song, Royal Albert Hall
National Canoe Exhibition, Crystal Palace
Pancake Race, Lincoln's Inn Fields

March
Oxford and Cambridge Boat Race, Putney to Mortlake
Head of River Races, Putney to Mortlake
Druid Ceremony, Tower Hill
Grimaldi Commemoration Service in honor of the clown, Holy Trinity Church, Dalston
Camden Festival (music and arts), Camden

Easter
St. Matthew Passion, St. Paul's Cathedral
Butterworth Charity (hot cross buns and money), St. Bartholomew the Great
Presentation by the Queen of Maundy Money (every 4 years), Westminster Abbey
Procession and Carols, Westminster Abbey
Easter Carnival Parade, Battersea Park
London Harness Horse Parade, Regent's Park

April
Westminster Cathedral Spring Flower Festival, Westminster
Beating the Bounds (as in boundary) of the Tower of London
Royal Horticultural Society Spring Flower Show, Royal Horticultural Society Halls, Westminster
London Marathon, Greenwich to Westminster
John Stow Commemoration Service, St. Andrew Undershaft
Signor Pasquale Favale's Marriage Portion, Guildhall
Shakespeare's Birthday Service, Southwark Cathedral

May
Royal Windsor Horse Show, Great Park, Windsor
Chelsea Flower Show, Royal Hospital, Chelsea
FA Cup Final, Wembley
London Private Fire Brigades Competition, Guildhall Yard
Lillies and Roses Ceremony, Tower of London
American Memorial Day, Cenotaph, Parliament Square, Westminster Abbey

May Day Rally, Hyde Park
Oak Apple Day Parade, Chelsea Pensioners, Royal Hospital, Chelsea

June
Garter Ceremony, Windsor Castle
Trooping of the Color Buckingham Palace, Horse Guards
Beating the Retreat, Horse Guards Parade, Whitehall
Charles Dickens Commemoration Service, Westminster Abbey
Greenwich Festival (arts, sports, music), Greenwich
All England Lawn Tennis Championships, Wimbledon
The Derby, Epsom Downs
Cricket Test Match, Lord's Cricket Ground
Royal Ascot, Berkshire

July
Royal International Horse Show, Wembley
Henry Wood Promenade Concerts, Royal Albert Hall
Benson and Hedges Cup Final, Lord's Cricket Ground
Doggett's Coat and Badge Race, London Bridge to Chelsea Bridge
The City Festival, City Churches and Halls
Swan-Upping, Temple Stairs at Tower Bridge, Henley
Lambeth Country Show, Brockwell Park
Mall March, Mall Horse Guards
Metropolitan Police Horse Show and Tournament, Imber Court, East Molesey

August
Hampstead Heath Fair, Hampstead Heath
Greater London Horse Show, Clapham Common
Presentation of a Boar's Head, Smithfield
Children's Books of the Year Show, National Book League
European Festival of Model Railways, Central Hall, Westminster
Test Match, Oval Cricket Ground
Notting Hill Festival, around Portobello Road

September
Election of the Lord Mayor, Guildhall, Mansion House
Battle of Britain Day, Greater London, Westminster Abbey
British Gymnastics Championships, Wembley

October
Horse of the Year Show, Wembley
National Brass Band's Championship, Royal Albert Hall
Opening of Michaelmas Law Term: Procession of Judges, Westminster Abbey
Quits Rents Ceremony, Law Courts
Harvest-of-the-Sea Thanksgiving, St. Mary-at-Hill
Trafalgar Day Ceremony, Trafalgar Square

November
Remembrance Sunday, Cenotaph, Whitehall
Lord Mayor's Show, Guildhall, Strand, Law Courts
London Film Festival
State Opening of Parliament, Buckingham Palace, House of Lords, Westminster
Guy Fawkes Night (with fireworks), Battersea Park, Crystal Palace Park, Burgess Park
Veteran Car Run, Hyde Park Corner, Brighton

December
Lighting of the Norwegian Christmas Tree, Trafalgar Square
Tower of London Parade, Tower of London
Midnight Eucharist, Southwark Cathedral
Watch-night Service, St. Paul's Cathedral
Watch-night Service, Westminster Abbey
Winter Ice Show, Wembley Arena
New Year's Eve Celebrations, Trafalgar Square

Kidding Around with John Muir Publications

We are making the world more accessible for young travelers. In your hand, you have one of several John Muir Publications guides written and designed especially for kids. We will be *Kidding Around* other cities also. Send us your thoughts, corrections, and suggestions. We also publish other books about travel and other subjects. Let us know if you would like one of our catalogs.

OTHER TITLES
AVAILABLE

COMING SOON

Kidding Around Los Angeles
Kidding Around New York City
Kidding Around Atlanta

John Muir Publications
P.O. Box 613
Santa Fe, New Mexico 87504
(505) 982-4078